Julian la araña blanca y hambrienta
Por David Darseli Santana

Ilustradores de artes visuales:

- **A**rtisto **W**ork (Principal #1 y creador principal de obras de arte)

- **D**avid **D**. **S**antana (Principal #2 y Editor Final de Arte)

- **M**arcos **I**gnacio Santana (Principal #3 y creador principal de colorización)

ESCENARIO DE LA ERA DEL ARTE Y CONCEPTUALIZACIÓN DE PERSONAJES POR...LA AMABLE Y BUENA RAIZ DE DIOS:

- **M**aría **L**uisa **A**viléz **F**ierro **L**arrinaga **d**e **M**edellín

Todas las ilustraciones y la historia (C) David Darseli Santana, Darseli Book Publishing. Reservados todos los derechos.

Abogado de David Darseli Santana y Darseli Book Publishing:

Oficina Legal de Dinah Perez, P.C.
1801 Century Park Este, Suite 2400
Los Ángeles, CA 90067

Ninguna parte de este libro puede reproducirse, almacenarse en un sistema de recuperación o transmitirse de ninguna forma ni por ningún medio, ya sea electrónico, mecánico, fotocopiado, grabación, Internet o cualquier otro sin el permiso legal expreso por escrito y notariado de los propietarios de los derechos de autor.

Julian The White Hungry Spider (ESPAÑOL) ISBN: **978-0-9896914-1-3**
Número de serie de identificación del editor:
2022DBPJULIAN1968MARCHSPANISH-PF

Agradecimientos: Un agradecimiento especial a **wework** y sus principales fundadores Miguel McKelvey, Adam Neumann y la esposa de Adam, Rebekah Victoria Neumann Paltrow. Su visión combinada creó un ambiente de trabajo divertido y propicio... ¡donde uno se siente inspirado por todos los que trabajan a su alrededor para lograr sus objetivos personales también! Aunque la historia y todas las ilustraciones se crearon en mis hogares, mis ediciones finales de 2022 de Julian The White Hungry Spider ocurrieron en **wework**. ¡Un aplauso para sus fundadores y todos los involucrados en ese momento y ahora por ir más allá en la creación de un entorno de "trabajo" tan excelente! ¡¡¡Vamos **wework**!!! Y, SOBRE TODO, Gracias A **Dios Padre** Por Amarnos Siempre.
....
Esta copia del libro es una copia del editor. Todas las copias de libros de este título son propiedad exclusiva de Publisher (Darseli Book Publishing). El acceso a este libro y cualquier libro de DBP y sus respectivas copias "medios" es SOLAMENTE mediante licencia. Para obtener acceso a este título, debe aceptar el Acuerdo de licencia de usuario final (también conocido como EULA) que se encuentra en las siguientes 3 páginas (y en los sitios web oficiales de Publisher). Tras la aceptación de este EULA y la compra de una licencia, puede obtener acceso a esta propiedad intelectual de DBP.

Lea atentamente las siguientes 3 páginas de EULA>>> para comprender cómo obtener acceso a una copia de Publisher de esta propiedad intelectual (puede encontrar un EULA actualizable en el sitio web de Publisher Darseli.Com O solicitándolo en: **MiCostaBella@Gmail.Com**).

Darseli Book Publishing's
Acuerdo de licencia de usuario final (EULA)

Contrato de licencia de usuario final (EULA) de Darseli Book Publishing (también conocido como DBP o Publisher). EULA también conocido como acuerdo de licencia o acuerdo o acuerdo de licencia de libros. LEA ESTE EULA y el siguiente EULA EN INGLÉS (ACUERDO DE LICENCIA DE DBP) CUIDADOSAMENTE ANTES DE COMPRAR UNA LICENCIA DE DBP PARA ACCEDER A ESTE PRODUCTO DE DBP Y EL papel propiedad del EDITOR (u otro) "MEDIO". Acuerdo de licencia de libros de DBP, también conocido como ACUERDO, LICENCIA, LICENCIA LIMITADA, Acuerdo de licencia de usuario final, CLUF y similares. Tras la aceptación completa de este acuerdo y la compra de una licencia DBP a partir de entonces, DBP le otorga una licencia limitada, personal, no exclusiva, intransferible y revocable (sin derecho a sublicencia) para acceder a este producto DBP específico (propiedad intelectual) y su correspondiente papel propiedad del Editor (o de otro modo) "Medio" relacionado con la licencia específica adquirida. Sin su ACEPTACIÓN COMPLETA de este acuerdo de licencia (EULA), no se le puede otorgar una emisión de (o mantener una licencia) para acceder a cualquier producto DBP y este producto DBP especificado y su PAPEL propiedad del Editor correspondiente (o de otro modo) "Medio" por el Editor. Por lo tanto, no tendrá acceso al producto DBP especificado o su "Medio" correspondiente. Este papel (o de otro modo) "Medio" (Copia propiedad del Editor) es en todo momento y lugar propiedad exclusiva del Editor y NO ESTÁ A LA VENTA. Solo se le otorga una licencia para acceder a la copia "Mediana" propiedad del Editor en cuanto a este EULA. Esta Licencia se interpretará como un acuerdo de licencia solamente, y cualquier derecho no otorgado expresamente en este documento está reservado por y para el Editor. Si necesita una traducción de cortesía de este EULA, envíe su solicitud a: MiCostaBella@Gmail.Com. Continúe leyendo el EULA completo en inglés para proceder a obtener o mantener una licencia activa para acceder a este y a cualquier producto de DBP y sus medios correspondientes:

Darseli Book Publishing's End User License Agreement (EULA)

Darseli Book Publishing (also known as DBP or Publisher) End User License Agreement (EULA). EULA also referred to as license agreement or book license agreement or agreement. PLEASE READ THIS EULA (DBP BOOK LICENSE AGREEMENT) CAREFULLY BEFORE PURCHASING a DBP LICENSE. DBP Book License Agreement also known as AGREEMENT, LICENSE, LIMITED LICENSE, End User License Agreement, EULA, and similar. Upon Full Acceptance of this agreement, and the purchase of a DBP license thereafter, DBP grants you a limited, personal, non-exclusive, non-transferable and revocable license (without the right to sublicense) to access a specified DBP product (intellectual property) and its respective and corresponding Publisher owned "Medium" related to the specific license purchased. Without your FULL ACCEPTANCE of this license agreement (EULA), an issuance of a license to access the DBP product specified and its corresponding Publisher owned "Medium" cannot be granted to you by the Publisher. Hence, you will not have access to the specified DBP product or its corresponding "Medium". This License shall be construed as a license agreement only, and any rights not expressly granted herein are reserved by and to the Publisher.

Specific DBP product in this License Agreement (but EULA pertains to any DBP product):
Julian la araña blanca y hambrienta   [Julian The Hungry Spider]

(hereinbefore and and hereinhere and hereafter referred to as book, the book, intellectual property, licensed intellectual property, DBP product, or similar references.):

International Standard Book Number (ISBN):
978-0-9896914-1-3

Publisher Identification Serial Number:
2022DBPJULIAN1968MARCH7SPANISH-PF

EULA SECTION ILA (Sec. 1 of 9): Introduction Agreement To License:

ILA 1: Darseli Book Publishing is hereinbefore and hereinhere and hereinafter referred to as, but not limited to: Publisher, us, our, DBP, Darseli Book Publishing, Grantor, intellectual property owner, author, Licensor, or similar references.

ILA 2: You the potential license buyer or purchaser or non-purchaser of the License to access the DBP product or book and its corresponding Publisher Owned "Medium" in this license agreement is referred to but not limited to: "I", the licensee, purchaser, you, your, and similar references.

ILA 3: By purchasing a license to access the DBP product or book (licensed intellectual property) listed above (or any DBP product) and its corresponding "Medium" you FULLY agree to the terms and conditions of this license agreement INCLUDING, WITHOUT LIMITATION, THE PROVISIONS ON LICENSE RESTRICTION, which began above and continues below. By your full agreement of this EULA you may purchase a license to come into access of a specified DBP product or book and its corresponding "Medium" (Medium owned perpetually by the Publisher).

ILA 4: Hereinbefore and hereinhere and hereinafter, the DBP product's or book's "Medium" refers to the medium used to house or place the intellectual property on such as but not limited to: paper medium, electronic medium, and so forth. If you came upon the book or its corresponding "Medium" without the purchase of a license, you are not authorize to use this intellectual property and its corresponding "Medium" which is property of the Publisher at all times and places. That is, the "Medium" (as well as the book or DBP product) remains at all times and places exclusive property of the Publisher. Accordingly, you Understand and Agree that this book and its "Medium" is NOT for SALE. The License purchased only grants you access to the book and its corresponding "Medium" in accordance to this EULA which describes among other items the restrictions of use of the book or DBP product and its corresponding "Medium".

ILA 5: You understand and agree that If you purchased the license to access a DBP product or book (intellectual property) and its corresponding "medium" format (paper or otherwise) and do not agree with the terms of this license agreement (EULA) after rereading them, return the intellectual property and its "Medium" within 34 days for a full LICENSE FEE refund (subject to DBP's Return Policy Found at Darseli.Com) TO THE PLACE WHERE YOU OBTAINED IT (be it either from the Publisher OR ITS AUTHORIZED AGENT (current DBP Authorized Agents listed at Darseli.Com, or by emailing us and requesting the current DBP Authorized Agents list to: MiCostaBella@Gmail.Com).

The DBP product or book and its corresponding "medium" MUST BE RETURNED at the time of refund request, and our authorization to do so, AND BEFORE REFUND in order to receive a LICENSE FEE refund. Shipping expense for the return of the licensed book and its "Medium" is at your expense if shipping is necessary. After the 34 days, NO REFUND of license fee is granted even if the Publisher terminates your license to use the book (DBP product) and its corresponding "Medium" for any reason including violation of this license agreement or suspected violation of this license agreement or for any other reason or for no reason.

Additionally, you understand and agree to re-read and FULLY agree to the full elaborate complete, and up to date EULA found at www.Darseli.Com, or by requesting the full current DBP EULA at MiCostaBella@Gmail.Com within 20 days of license purchase.

ILA 6-Sub 1: Full refund applies only to "PAPER" medium format or similar Tangible "Medium" format of the book (DBP product). Intangible format of the book (such as electronic "Medium" format of the book and similar) are NOT entitled for refund even if your license to use the book is terminated by Publisher for violation or suspected violation of the book license agreement or for any reason or no reason, or by your disagreement with the full book license agreement (EULA).

ILA 6-Sub 2: Accordingly, for such intangible "Medium" format such as "electronic" format (and tangible "Medium" formats such as "paper"), the Publisher STRONGLY advises the potential purchaser of a DBP license to CAREFULLY read the license agreement in full, understand it completely, and FULLY agree with it completely BEFORE purchasing a DBP license to access any DBP product and its corresponding "medium".

ILA 7: This is an agreement made between you, the entity in possession or to be in possession of our intellectual property and its corresponding "Medium" via the purchase of a license or the license purchaser or potential purchaser of the license or entity in possession of our book and its "Medium" (irrespective of being authorized or not) AND the Publisher of the DBP product or book.

ILA 8: An entity may not purchase a license to access the DBP product or book and its corresponding medium if the entity is not considered a legal adult in their country of origin where they are a citizen.

Minors living under the same physical residence of the legal adult purchaser of a DBP license, may access the DBP product or book and its corresponding "Medium" for personal use only and as outlined in this license agreement. The minor must be supervised at all times by the DBP license purchaser when using any DBP product including books and their corresponding medium. And the DBP license purchaser is responsible for the acts of the minor that go against the interest of the Publisher and its intellectual property and corresponding mediums and the EULA. You fully agree that Any violation by the minor against this EULA makes the purchaser of a DBP license and its corresponding medium fully liable. Purchaser is the DBP license buyer granted access to the DBP product or the book and its corresponding "Medium". The purchaser is also the entity that has agreed to this EULA and proceeded to purchase a DBP license to access the Publisher's intellectual property and its corresponding medium.

ILA 9: This license agreement to access the DBP product and its corresponding "Medium" is NOT a contract for sale and or rent of a DBP product or book or its corresponding "Medium": RATHER, it is a license to access and use a DBP product or book and its corresponding "Medium" subject to the terms and conditions of this Agreement (EULA). The DBP product or book and its corresponding "Medium" is licensed NOT SOLD.

ILA 10: You fully agree that The DBP product or book and its corresponding "Medium" (physical or non-physical) (in paper, plastic, electronic format, or otherwise) is always property of the Publisher and cannot be transferred by the licensee or third party or any other entity at anytime or place. You also understand and fully agree that the DBP product or book and its corresponding "Medium" provided is Not for you to give-away, sale, rent, license, sublicense, transfer, delegate, or otherwise at any time and at any location by you or a third party or any entity be it at a physical place, the Internet or otherwise (said items always remain exclusive property of the Publisher). You also fully agree that You are only granted a license to access and use the intellectual property and its "Medium" for personal use only and as to the terms of this agreement.

ILA 11: Please read the terms and conditions above and below carefully.

DBP and you agree on the above and the below sections and everything in it. If you do not FULLY agree with this EULA, you may not purchase a license to use any DBP product or book and its corresponding "Medium" or maintain the book and its corresponding "medium" in your possession. Furthermore, No entity may have in its/his/her possession any DBP product or book and its corresponding "Medium" without having a purchased Publisher granted license to access them unless otherwise stated in this EULA.

EULA SECTION NTI (Sec. 2 of 9):: Non-Transferable Disclosure (NTD)

NTD 1: You may have an additional notarized written agreement directly with Publisher (for example: a volume license agreement) that only supplements this agreement. You agree that In no way does any other written agreement with the Publisher contradict the core of this license agreement including the understanding that the publisher maintains at all times and places exclusive ownership of the DBP product or book and its corresponding "Medium", and you agree that the license restrictions and all other restrictions in this license agreement (EULA) are preserved in any other additional written agreement that may be made by the Publisher and you or other entity (including an entity that is granted status by the Publisher as an Authorized Agent of the Publisher).

NTD 2: Limited Rights. Upon payment of the nonrefundable DBP license fee (refundable only within 34 days as stated earlier for paper "medium" format only), you agree that DBP grants you a limited, non-exclusive, revocable, nontransferable license to use a particular respective DBP product or book (intellectual property) and its corresponding "Medium". You agree that any authorized agent granted by the Publisher must follow the core outline of this EULA as well at all times.

EULA SECTION NDPA (Sec. 3 of 9): No Distribution Permitted Agreement (NDPA):

NDPA 1: This Agreement describes the terms governing your use of the DBP product or book (intellectual property), intellectual property content, and the corresponding "Medium" in any format.

NDPA 2A: You and any other entity further and additionally FULLY agree, understand, and accept that the United States (U.S.) Copyright Law SECTION § 109, and also in particular its (§ 109) subsection (a) and (c) (or any other nation similar section) do not apply to this agreement or any DBP product; and you and any other entity who may be in possession of a DBP product or the book and or its corresponding "Medium" understand and agree not to use this said Copyright section to contradict this EULA, since this DBP product or book and its corresponding "Medium" are licensed and not sold.

NDPA 2B: Furthermore, you agree that as to this section, and subsection (d), of aforementioned U.S. Copyright Law, you are not permitted to post or sale or give-away or otherwise on the Internet or any other medium of communication or platform, or anywhere or place any DBP product and its "medium" without the exclusive notarized written authorization of the copyright owner and Publisher. That is, as to this EULA and its corresponding DBP product or book and its "Medium", The privileges prescribed by subsections (a) and (c) and (d) [of U.S. Copyright Section §109] do not apply to any DBP product and its "Mediums" since DBP products are licensed Not Sold and your privileges to access our DBP products and books and its "Medium" are limited as described in this EULA.

NDPA 3A: You understand and agree that the granted license, DBP products or this book, and its corresponding "Medium" CANNOT, at no time or place, by you or any other entity (besides the Publisher and a specified notarized authorized DBP Agent) be leased, licensed, sub-licensed, loaned, assign, conveyed, transferred, copied, reproduced, modified, adapted, merged, translated, given-away, rented, displayed and or announced to the public in any platform or way, or sold or otherwise distributed in any way, shape, form or format by you or any entity other than the Publisher and its specified notarized authorized DBP Agent, or as specified in this EULA.

You agree that Only the Publisher and the Publisher's designated Publisher Authorized Agents of any DBP product may provide distribution of "license" of DBP products or this book
and its corresponding "Medium" in accordance to this license agreement.

NDPA 3B: PROPRIETARY RIGHTS: Except where specifically stated otherwise in this EULA, you understand and agree that DBP owns all rights, titles and interest in and to all DBP products and their corresponding Medium including, without limitation, all intellectual and proprietary rights appurtenant thereto, and, except for the limited license granted to you herein, nothing in this EULA shall be construed to transfer, convey, impair or otherwise adversely affect DBP and its authors et al. ownership or proprietary rights therein or any other DBP information or materials, tangible or intangible, in any form and in any medium. All intellectual property rights, including copyright, patents, trademarks and trade secrets, are retained by the Publisher and its affiliates, licensors, and collaborators, all rights reserved.

You understand and agree that you may not copy, imitate or use the Trademarks et al., in whole or in part, for any purpose. No license or other right to use any Trademark et al. used or displayed on any of our mediums or marketing material is granted to You.

NDPA 3C: You understand and agree that **you may always view the Current List of Authorized Agents of DBP on its website or you can request a Current list at: MiCostaBella@Gmail.Com.** You further understand and agree that you will check the Current list of authorized Agents of DBP, before purchasing a DBP license, to make sure you are buying your license legally before you purchase any DBP license to access any DBP product and its corresponding medium.

NDPA 4-sub 1: You understand and agree and will honor that Darseli Book Publishing holds exclusive distribution rights of its products and corresponding mediums on any platform, the INTERNET or other electronic market places or similar electronic devises in addition to all non-Internet platforms.

You understand and agree that An editorial review or other similar opinion may reference the intellectual property in an article or news feed only so far as it does not imply any monetary gain for entity providing such news feed or book review article. Written request to do so can be made to the Publisher at: MiCostaBella@Gmail.Com. The exception would be a notarized written agreement with the Publisher in advance.

NDPA 4-sub 2: You understand and agree that All authorized license distribution Authorized Agent entities must agree with DBP on a Separate notarized written Agreement before the distribution entity is authorized to distribute any DBP license (including the DBP product's corresponding Publisher's medium {physical or non-physical cover and pages in paper format and/or electronic format, or otherwise containing a particular DBP product}) on behalf of the Publisher, and only after the granted distribution agent entity is on the "CURRENT AND UP-TO-DATE" DBP Authorized Agent List posted at Darseli.com website or by request of current agent list to MiCostaBella@Gmail.Com. This Agent List fluctuates (CHANGES) and so it is recommended to check the Updated Authorized DBP Agent List as indicated BEFORE DEALING WITH an apparent Publisher Authorized Agent or to make sure you are dealing with a Current and Valid Publisher Authorized Agent. Publisher Authorized License Reseller can be terminated by the Publisher at any time for any reason, especially in a violation of this EULA or its agreed commitments to DBP and general business integrity and ethical standards.

EULA SECTION LGR (Sec. 4 of 9): License Grant And Restrictions (LGR):

LGR 1-sub-1: YOU agree you will Not Transfer your license, lease or sublease your license, rent or license or sublicense your license, sale your license, assign your license, delegate or transfer or give-away your license rights of any DBP product, book (or e-book),or its Publisher owned "Medium" in any way or format or time or place (or in any format that may be conceived now or in the future). That is, you understand and agree that this limited DBP license is granted to you and you alone (license is exclusive to you only).

LGR 1-sub-2: YOU agree you will Not authorize another individual or entity to copy, reproduce, modify, adapt, merge, translate, assign, transfer or otherwise any DBP product or book and its corresponding "Medium" onto any computer or any other platform.

LGR 1-sub-3: You further agree and understand that the license granted to you pertains to only one corresponding DBP product and its corresponding "Medium" and no more. If you wish to purchase an additional license to have access to another single corresponding DBP product or book (and its "Medium"), you understand and agree that you must purchase another (separate) license to do so (allowing you access to that license's single corresponding book and DBP product and its corresponding "Medium").

LGR 2-sub-1: The book or DBP product is licensed to you generally for the "life" of the corresponding physical or electronic, or otherwise "Medium" or as to a specified time given by the Publisher at the time of ordering or acquiring from the Publisher or Publisher's authorized agent (so long as you abide by the EULA) as to this EULA or immediately terminate access if Publisher decides to revoke your license (and access to its corresponding DBP product and Medium) for any reason.

LGR 2-sub-2: You understand and agree that this license is revocable and can be Terminated by the Publisher at any time for any reason and without notice to you. Reason for termination may include your violation of this agreement or suspected violation of this agreement. At such time, you agree to surrender the book and its "Medium" (which is property of the Publisher at all times and places) to the Publisher or immediately destroy it if Publisher asks you to do so.

LGR 2-sub-3: You understand and agree that if you are No Longer interested in the DBP product or book during the period specified in the granted DBP product license, you acknowledge and agree that you will destroy the book and its corresponding "Medium" (or if e-Book or similar "Medium" format: delete the electronic file or similar file of the DBP product and its corresponding "Medium" provided).

LGR2-sub-4: You understand and agree that a DBP license purchaser can obtain their unique DBP license number by adding in sequence the unique DBP license serial number components using the following DBP license identifiers:

(1) The word or symbol "DBP" at beginning,
(2) followed by the YEAR, MONTH, DAY of DBP License purchase date,
(3) followed by one Family Name of DBP product license Purchaser,
(4) followed by the number of DBP licenses ordered in numerical digits (2 or more licenses listed as A1, B1, C1,... Ax, Bx, Cx,etc.)
(5) The DBP license Purchaser's Country of Origin as indicated,
(6) followed by the numerical date: 4-13-1950,
(7) and followed by and ended with the first (non-article) Word in the title of the corresponding DBP product.

You further agree that if the Publisher asks for this DBP license number, you will furnish it to the Publisher as an authentication of your DBP product license purchase. Accordingly, you agree to write this DBP product license number somewhere secure where you can access it if need be. **You also understand and agree that we may ask, and you will provide, additional identifiers to verify that you are the actual purchaser of the DBP product license.**

LGR 3: You agree that you are never allowed to obtain any tangible or intangible monetary or similar benefits for sharing unless otherwise specified in this EULA.

LGR 4: You further understand and agree that Only the Publisher or the Publisher's Authorized Agents (current authorized agents posted on the current DBP list at Darseli.Com or by request at MiCostaBella@Gmail.Com) are allowed to distribute a DBP product license, the DBP product and its corresponding license-only Publisher "Medium" which belongs to Publisher at all times and places.

LGR 5: Non-Profit public libraries (herein herewith also known as "public library" or "public libraries" or "library" or "libraries") are the ONLY ENTITY permitted in this license agreement to allow their patrons to check out "share" the book and its "medium", FREE OF CHARGE, as a form of sharing the book so long as the book is returned to the original licensed entity (the public library that purchased a corresponding license to a single corresponding book from the Publisher).

LGR 5 sub-1: Aforementioned Libraries CANNOT sell, lease, sublease, license, sub-license, give away, rent, rent for monetary gain, copy, reproduce, modify, adapt, or otherwise the License, the book or DBP product, and its corresponding "Medium" at ANYTIME for any reason including if the public library decides to discard the book and its "Medium": in such cases the book (or DBP product) and its corresponding "Medium" must be destroyed by the library holding a corresponding DBP license, or return, at its expense, to the Publisher the DBP product and its corresponding Medium. If the said medium is in electronic or similar format, the library agrees to delete or otherwise destroy the DBP product's licensed medium.

LGR 7 sub-2A: All other restrictions in this DBP product license agreement apply directly to public libraries as well. If the public library does not agree fully with this EULA or any part of this agreement, they are not permitted to purchase a license of a DBP product or book or to acquire (by any means) a DBP product or the book and its corresponding "Medium".

LGR 8: EDUCATOR PRIVILEGES as to a DBP license: A credentialed, certificated educator may share the book or DBP product and its corresponding medium with his or her assigned students during school hours within the school on-site physical classroom. Students must be supervised at all time by the DBP license purchaser (educator) when using any DBP product including books and their corresponding medium. Students may not borrow the book as it is to remain with the educator (who purchased the DBP product license) at all times. And said DBP license purchaser is responsible for the acts of the students that go against the interest of the Publisher and its intellectual property and corresponding mediums and the EULA. The "Educator" DBP license purchaser understands and agrees that Any violation by students against this EULA makes the "EDUCATOR" purchaser of a DBP license fully liable.

LGR 9: The DBP product License does not allow the DBP product to be used on more than one "Medium" other than that provided to you by the Publisher or its authorized agent at time of license purchase, and you understand and agree that you may not make the book or DBP product available over additional physical "Medium" formats or electronic "Medium" formats or any other type of "Medium" formats or any type of network where it could be used by multiple people or devices or multiple computers at the same time or stand-alone. This DBP product License does not grant you any rights to share the DBP issued license, the book or DBP product and its corresponding "Medium" other than those explicitly stated in this Agreement.

EULA SECTION T (Sec. 5 of 9): Termination (T1)

T1: The Publisher, Darseli Book Publishing, may, at its sole discretion and without notice, terminate your DBP product license for ANY REASON effective immediately. Such license termination by the Publisher terminates your access to use the single corresponding DBP product and its corresponding "Medium" (Medium owned by the Publisher at all times and places). Upon Termination stated, you understand and agree that you are not entitled to any compensation or refund of any kind due to said termination or otherwise. You also agree that Upon termination of your license by Publisher you must immediately stop using the book or DBP product and its "Medium" and destroy the DBP product and its corresponding "Medium", or return them to the Publisher (at your own shipping expense). If the book or DBP product and its "Medium" is in digital format or similar format, then you are instructed to immediately delete the DBP product and its corresponding "medium" from your hard drive or other storage mechanism or constructs or otherwise upon termination of your license.

T2: If in turn you wish to terminate (end) an issued license and this license agreement of a DBP product or book (such termination by you effectively and immediately terminates your access to the book or DBP product and its corresponding "Medium"), you must immediately destroy or return (at your own shipping expense) to Publisher the book and its "Medium" as described above. The balance of the Agreement shall survive any such 'termination of license rights'. You are not entitled to a license fee refund upon termination unless specified differently in this license agreement.

EULA SECTION LPMA (Sec. 6 of 9): License Fee Payment And Modification Agreement (LPMA):

LPMA 1: You agree and understand that the DBP product license to be issued to you (and possession of its single corresponding book and its Publisher's "medium"), upon and after your agreement of this EULA license agreement, requires payment to the Publisher or its authorized agent at the current set "License Fee" amount, or license fee amount presented to you, for the completion of a DBP product license issuance to you.

LPMA 2: Certain book or DBP product license issuances by Publisher to particular individuals or organizations are granted without a license fee for the sole purpose of promotional review of the book and its "Medium". Such granted DBP product licenses to these particular individuals or organizations by the Publisher are also bound to this license agreement and its sections in its entirety (which includes non-transferable rules of the license, the book or its Publisher owned "Medium" or selling of book or DBP product or otherwise transferring DBP products in violation of this DBP product license agreement). If aforementioned particular entity receiving from the Publisher such a DBP product license with its corresponding book and its "medium" in this way does not fully agree with this EULA license agreement, then their granted license is immediately revoked and they agree that they must immediately return (at their shipping expense) or destroy their provided licensed DBP product and its corresponding "Medium", and all other parts of this license agreement survive.

LPMA 3: You understand and agree that The Publisher reserves the right to modify this agreement (EULA) at any time to reflect, for example but not limited to, and without notice, changes in our business or to maintain a DBP product or book in a license ONLY format. If DBP modifies this EULA agreement a revised version will be posted on our website www.darseli.com and/or our official social web pages or you may request the current EULA by email to: MiCostaBella@Gmail.Com. You agree that your continued use of any of our DBP products and books and their corresponding "Medium" will constitute your acceptance of the modified agreement that can be made at any time and without notice other than posting a revised agreement on one of our official web pages or our other public notice platforms at our option or by you requesting a revised EULA via email as stated.

If you do not agree with the DBP revised license agreement (EULA) changes allowing you to have continued access to any of our DBP products or books and their respective corresponding "Medium" in your possession or to be in your possession, you herewith agree to destroy or return the DBP product and its corresponding "Medium" (shipping expense belongs to you) to the Publisher (or its authorized agent) without a refund or any other sort of compensation to you.

EULA SECTION LLLA (Sec. 7 of 9): Language and Law Of License Agreement (LLLA):

LLLA 1: The controlling language of this agreement is in English ONLY. Any translation of this license agreement to any other language besides English that you may have received is provided only for your convenience. You understand and agree If any discrepancies are found in language translation of this EULA, the controlling language of this EULA is English always.

LLLA 2A: Controlling Law and Severability: This license is to be governed by the State of Washington, U.S.A. If any part of this agreement is found void and unenforceable by a legitimate government entity court, it will not affect the validity of the balance of this agreement, which will remain valid and enforceable according to its terms. This agreement may only be modified in writing by the Publisher: Darseli Book Publishing (DBP). Again, the English version of this agreement will be the ONLY version used when interpreting or construing this agreement.

LLLA 2B: You irrevocably and unconditionally (a) consent to submit to the exclusive jurisdiction of the state and federal courts of King County, Washington for any litigation or disputed arising out of or related to this Agreement, (b) you agree not to commence any litigation arising out of or related to this Agreement except in the state or federal courts mentioned herein, (c) you agree not to plead or claim that such litigation brought therein has been brought in an inconvenient forum. (d) EACH PARTY (you and the Publisher and any other unforeseen entity) HEREBY WAIVES ITS RIGHT TO A JURY TRIAL IN CONNECTION WITH ANY DISPUTE OR LEGAL PROCEEDING ARISING OUT OF THIS AGREEMENT OR THE SUBJECT MATTER HEREOF AND THEREOF.

LLLA 3: COMPLIANCE WITH EXPORT LAWS. You may not use or otherwise export or re-export any DBP product except as authorized by the Publisher and the United States law and the laws of the jurisdiction in which the DBP product was obtained. In particular, but without limitation, any DBP product may not be exported or re-exported (a) into any U.S. embargoed countries or (b) to anyone on the U.S. Treasury Department's list of Specially Designated Nationals or the U.S. Department of Commerce Denied Person's List or Entity List. By using any DBP product as licensed to you and specified in this EULA, you represent and warrant that you are not located in any such country or on any such list. You also agree that you will not use any DBP product for any purposes prohibited by United States of America law.

LLLA 4: The DBP product License Provided by Authorized Third Parties:

The Publisher does not control, endorse, or accept responsibility for Any third party services. Any dealings between you and any authorized or unauthorized third party in connection with a Third Party Service or sell, including such party's privacy policies and use of your personal information, delivery of and payment for licenses fees and services, and any other terms, conditions, warranties, or representations associated with such dealings, are solely between you and such third party. Any DBP authorized third party agent must always abide by DBP's EULA and additional notarized agreements between authorized 3rd Party Agent and DBP. Any third party Authorized distributor of a DBP product license, as an agent for the Publisher, agrees to abide by its separate agreement with Publisher and also to abide by the Publisher's EULA outlined here. No third party is permitted to violate any Publisher sections in this agreement. Furthermore, any agent of the Publisher is to abide by all laws in the region in which it resides in so far as it does not violate this license agreement and the additional separate license agreement with Publisher. If you purchased a license of a DBP product via an authorized 3rd Party DBP agent and cannot find a suitable resolution to your issue, please bring it up directly to the Publisher at MiCostaBella@Gmail.Com. The Publisher will do its best to attempt to resolve your issue.

LLLA 5: Equitable Relief. You hereby fully agree that any breach of this Agreement by you, including any unauthorized disclosure of Confidential Information or specific sections in this Agreement, would cause irreparable harm to the Publisher, and that in the event of any breach or threatened breach of this agreement, The Publisher will be entitled to obtain equitable relief in addition to any other remedy. Publisher's rights and remedies under this Agreement shall be cumulative and not exclusive of any other rights or remedies provided hereunder or by law.

EULA SECTION OA (Sec. 8 of 9):: Other Agreements (OA)

OA 1: Indemnity. You, and or possessor of DBP products and their corresponding "Mediums", agree to defend and indemnify and hold harmless the Publisher (DBP) and its authors and employees or contracted employees, officers, directors, agents, successors, assigns, and affiliates from any and all liabilities, losses, actions, damages, settlements, or claims (including all reasonable expenses, costs, and attorneys' fees) out of or relating to your use of, or any reliance on, any DBP products including this DBP product and its corresponding "Medium" or service of a DBP product. Your use of any DBP products including this DBP product and its corresponding "Medium" are used AT YOUR OWN RISK.

OA 3: Intellectual Property Rights; No Modifications. You acknowledge and agree that this and any DBP product and its corresponding "Medium", and the trademarks associated with the DBP product, and its corresponding "Medium" are the intellectual property owned by the Publisher (DBP), and/or the author of the DBP product or book or its illustrators. DBP, the authors, et al. reserve all of their respective rights under such applicable laws. All DBP products are protected by Copyright, Trademark, et al., including without limitation, by United States Copyright Law, international treaty provisions, and applicable laws in the jurisdiction of use.

EULA SECTION G (Sec. 9 of 9): General (G):

G 1: This license Agreement of the specified DBP product or any DBP product, herewith, herein, including Additional Terms below, is the Entire Agreement between you (the licensee or to be licensee (or entity in possession of a DBP product) granted access to the DBP product by way of DBP license with license fee payment made or otherwise acquired) and the Publisher (DBP): and replaces all prior understandings, communications and agreements, oral or written (with the exception of additional notarized Agent-Publisher separate agreement or other notarized agreement with the Publisher). If any court of law, having the jurisdiction, rules that any part of this Agreement is not consistent with its laws: that part of the that agreement will be formally removed without affecting the remainder of the License Agreement (EULA) which shall continue in full force and effect.

G 2: Additionally, You understand and agree that if the Publisher does not agree with a court of law decision, the Publisher may revoke your license and henceforth end your privilege to any DBP product (intellectual property) and its corresponding "Medium". In such an event, the licensee entity of a DBP product or holder of the corresponding "medium" of the DBP product, you, shall immediately return (at licensee's and or holder's own shipping expense) or destroy the DBP product and its corresponding "medium" in its, her, his possession immediately.

G 2-sub 1: You understand and agree that The United Nations Convention on Contracts for the International Sale of Goods does Not apply to this Agreement (the application of which is expressly excluded). You cannot loan, assign, delegate, sell, rent, convey, transfer, copy, reproduce, modify, adapt, merge, translate or otherwise dispose of, whether voluntarily or involuntarily, by operation of law or otherwise, or transfer ownership of this Agreement and license (AND its book and corresponding Publisher's owned "Medium") to anyone without written approval from the Publisher or as instructed in this EULA. However, the Publisher may assign or transfer license (and its corresponding book and "Medium") without your consent or notice to an authorized affiliate, similar, or whom ever the Publisher wishes to designate at any time and place.

G 3: UNIQUE LICENSE NUMBER. Each DBP product and its corresponding "Medium" has a unique license number (as described earlier in this EULA). The license number is set to correspond directly to a purchaser of the license in order to access the single corresponding book and its Publisher owned "Medium". This Unique License number is also kept at the Publisher's Databases corresponding to an exact purchaser of a DBP product license. That is, the License is a unique 1 to 1 correspondence: Publisher granting license and corresponding license number to One Licensee corresponding to a single DBP product and its corresponding Publisher owned "Medium". This license number is non-transferable at any time or place unless otherwise stated in this agreement. And, you understand and agree that you are to keep this license number Confidential for security reasons between the Publisher and You.

G 3 sub-1: If the "medium" of any DBP product comes into a possession of someone or an entity other than the original purchaser of the license, it is here advised that such entity in possession of any DBP product and its corresponding "medium" is not allowed to access the DBP product (intellectual property) or its corresponding Publisher owned "medium". Henceforth, such an entity without authorization to access a DBP product is herewith advised to immediately destroy the DBP product and its corresponding "medium" to avoid legal remedies on behalf of the Publisher for violation of the book's EULA, licensing only distribution format, and other legal rights.

G4: This EULA license agreement wording ends on this written line.

Este libro está dedicado a

María Luisa Aviléz Fierro Larrinaga de Medellín

... una persona cariñosa que se preocupaba y ayudaba a quienquiera que encontraba. Ella también fue una devota madre y suegra.

....María Luisa fue un ser humano que trabajó incansablemente para proveer sus 6 hijos: (Elizabeth, Nannette, Cecilia, Diana, Alfonso y Bernardo).

...un maravilloso ser humano que no solo ayudó a su familia sino también su prójimo a quien llegó a conocer. Ella ayudó especialmente las personas sin hogar de Santa Mónica, California.

...Ella fue una artista visual que ayudó con la primera conceptualización visual de este libro infantil: **Julian la araña blanca y hambrienta** [Julian the White Hungry Spider].

¡Gracias Abi!

Al igual que Abi, el autor de este libro encuentra formas de tratar de ayudar a la humanidad también.

Recientemente, el autor se encontró con una organización humanitaria que busca mitigar los males del sufrimiento humano encontrando, con otros, soluciones viables y proponiendo estas soluciones a las comunidades. Lo bueno de esta organización. es que no acepta ninguna contribución económica. Todos los costos asociados con los esfuerzos de la organización son pagados por separado y directamente por los miembros ellos mismos de acuerdo a su capacidad y voluntad.

Para ver lo que descubrió el autor y posiblemente unirse, vaya a:

Eternoi.Com
Eternoi Humanitarian Organization (Eternoi)

Había una vez una araña blanca que estaba **constantemente** hambrienta. La araña blanca llamada **Julián** vivía en una pequeña caja en la habitación de un niño.

Durante días la araña tenía HAMBRE.

Un día, debido a su hambre, la araña blanca decidió salir de la caja y comenzar su BÚSQUEDA de comida.

Cuando la araña blanca caminó sobre sus *ocho patas largas* por la caja y por un pequeño agujero en la parte superior, vio comida. Era un sándwich de jalea de fresa con pan blanco en una pequeña mesa de madera al lado de una cama pequeña.

¡Guauu! Se ve impresionante!
¡ Oh mi J !

La araña blanca subió la pequeña mesa de madera. Mientras ponía los ojos en el sándwich de jalea, **saboreaba** cada parte.

La araña blanca nunca había comido un sándwich de jalea y tenía miedo de comerlo por **TEMOR** a que lo enfermara. Sin embargo, tenía tanta hambre que no tenía importancia: tomó su primer bocado. Después de la primera mordida, rápidamente comió el resto del bocadillo de jalea hasta que no quedó ¡¡NADA!!!:)
　　　　　　　　　　　　　　　NADA LEFT!!!!:)
　　　　　　　　　　　　　　　NADA RIGHT!!!:)

¡ERUCTAAAR!

Comer toda esta comida hizo que la araña blanca se pusiera GORDA y **REDONDA**. Mientras **bajaba** lentamente por la mesa, su cuerda de araña empezaba a **romper** a causa de **todo-el-peso** que Julian (la araña blanca) había ganado comiendo TODO el bocadillo.

Cuando **bajó** completamente del aire, caminó lentamente por la habitación y volvió a su casa en la caja.:) [satisfecho hey Julian!:)]

¡Pero cuando llegó a la caja, no podía encajar en el agujero que usaba como puerta! Estaba TAN GORDO y red**O**nd**O** que el agujer**O** ya no era lo suficientemente grande como para C A B E **R**rrrr.

Julian se sentó en la parte superior de la caja pensando en el tema. Después de un tiempo, se le ocurrió una idea. Su idea era **detener su respiración** en el tiempo suficiente para permitirle encajar **A TRAVÉS DEL** agujer**O** (que era aproximadamente del tamaño de un níquel norte-norte americano).

Después de una larga lucha, Julián finalmente se **ESTRUJÓ** a través del ¡¡¡¡**aguj**er**OoooOO**. **agu agu agu:)**!!!

Cuando Julián desapareció en silencio, Marcos (el niño que vivía en la habitación) entró en la habitación. ¡Cuando aLCANZÓ su sándwich de jalea
no agarró NADA!
NOTHING!!!!
¡NADA!

-¿Qué le pasó a mi sándwich? -**gritó**-. Marcos se sorprendió y luego se **enfadó** por la desaparición de su sándwich. "¿Quién podría haber tomado mi sándwich?" Se preguntó. Finalmente llegó a la conclusión de que su madre lo había tomado por accidente. Decidió olvidarse del sándwich y se fue a dormir. ¡*mir mir mir*!

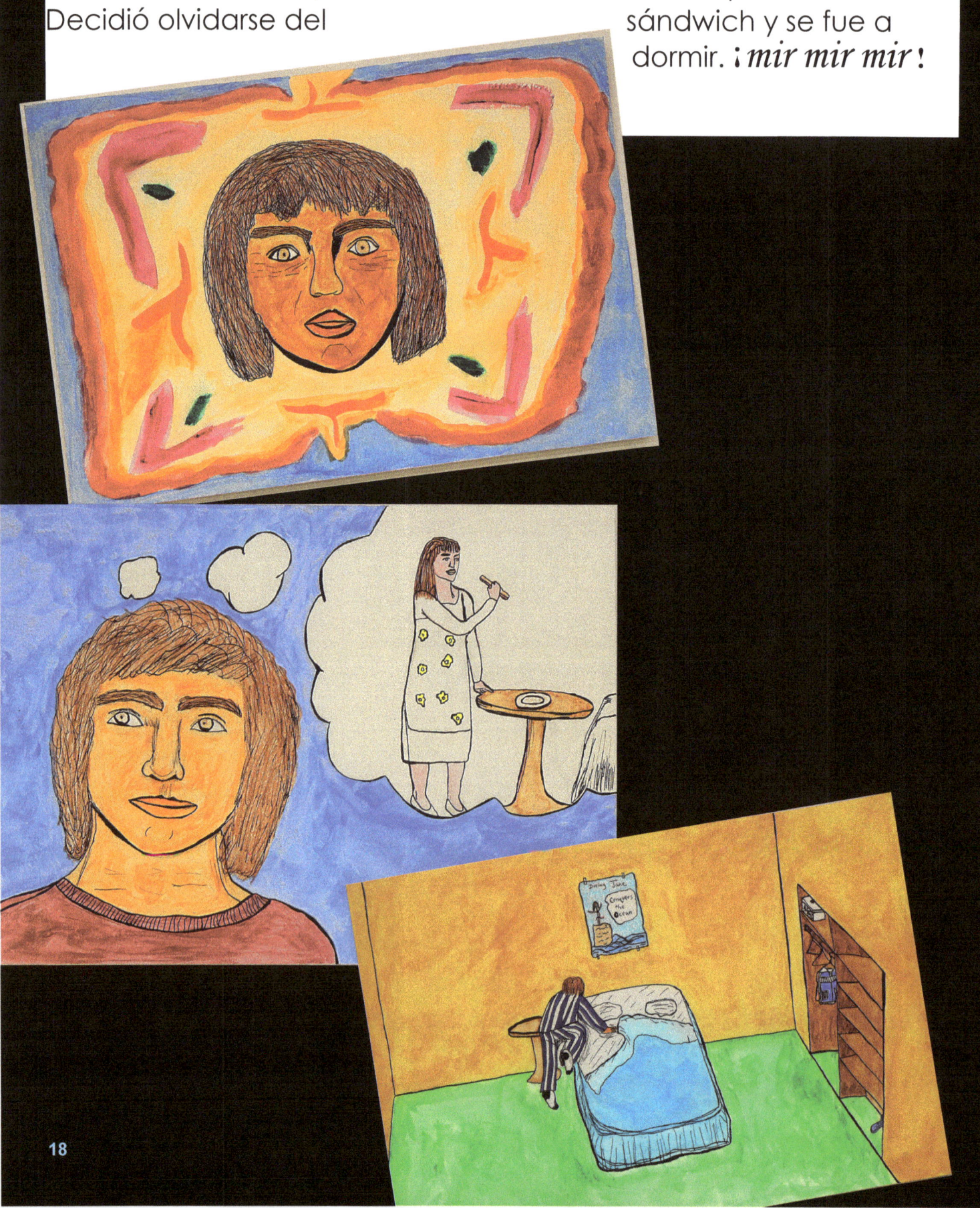

Al día siguiente sucedió LO MISMO cuando estaba en el baño. Esta vez estaba **muy molesto** porque realmente quería comer su sándwich de jalea **antes** de irse a dormir. Marcos decidió *bajar* las escaleras para hablar con su madre sobre la desaparición de su sándwich de jalea.

Cuando llegó a la cocina, su madre estaba lavando los platos de la tarde. "¡Mamá! ¿Tomaste mi sándwich de jalea de mi habitación? ", Le preguntó él con **severidad**. Su madre respondio: "No Marcos, no lo hice. ¿Por qué? ". Marcos respondio: " ¡Por la segunda noche consecutiva ha desaparecido! Había dejado mi sándwich de jalea en mi pequeña mesa de madera mientras yo usaba el baño. Cuando volví a mi habitación, mi sándwich de jalea había DESAPARECIDO !!! ":(

-Tal vez comiste el bocadillo antes de ir al baño -dijo pensativo su madre-. Marcos **protestó**: "¡No podría haber ocurrido **DOS VECES SEGUIDAS** sin que yo me diera cuenta de ello **mamá!**" Una **duda comenzó a CRECER en** Marcos. El niño luego dijo (TRATANDO de *calmarse*): "Bueno ... Podría haber sucedido como usted dice. Intentaré ser más consciente de ello mañana ". Con eso dicho, Marcos se fue **a dormir**.

Al tercer día, mientras Marcos iba al baño, se recordó a sí mismo que su bocadillo **seguía** sobre la mesa.

Cuando regresó a su habitación su sandwich había desaparecido!

El niño se puso m**uuuy furioso** y GRITÓ: "¿¡Quién comió mi sándwich!?" Nadie respondió. Julian (la araña blanca) había regresado a su casa en la caja **antes de que** Marcos regresara **del baño.** Julián no entendía la comunicación HUMANA. Los sonidos que hacía el niño eran sólo **V I B R A CIONES** que venían desde **FUERA** de la caja.

Marcos el niño entonces decidió poner ¡una trampa para el ladrón! "¡Mañana veremos **quién** se va arrepentir!", dijo Marcos mientras pensaba Traviosamente en su plan.

Mientras tanto, Julián no se sentía bien. Tenía dolor en el estómago. "**Aaauu-Ouch !, aaauuu0-¡Ah !, ¡ay!**" Se quejó. "¿Tal vez comí **demasiado**?", Pensó Julián la araña. Continuó pensando: "Pero no podría haber sido **demasiado** ya que normalmente como un sándwich de jalea ENTERA.", Agregó Julián en **¡idioma de *araña*!**

Después de un rato de pensar en el asunto: un idea se le vino. "¡Sé lo que es! Es la **mantequilla-de-cacahuete** que estaba en el sándwich de jalea. **Uuuu-Ooooo-¡No!** ", Gruñó tristemente. "Nunca comeré un sándwich de jalea si tiene **mantequilla-de-maní** en ella **!Yucky yuck yuck!** "

Por la mañana, después de VOMITAR e ir al baño muchas veces durante la noche, Julián se sintió mejor. [!buenas noticias Julián!]

Tarde in el cuarto día, Julián **bajó** de la caja y caminó hacia el sándwich de jalea: que estaba sobre la pequeña mesa de madera junto a la cama de Marcos el niño.

Cuando se acercó al bocadillo, Julián la araña pudo OLER la **mantequilla-de-cacahuete.** "**No, no, no, NO! ¡No voy a comer esto!** ", Dijo Julián. Así que volvió a la caja SIN comer.

Cuando Marcos el niño regresó a su habitación (desde el baño), se dio cuenta de que todo en la mesa seguía **IGUAL**. La **TRAMPA** que había colocado **de**$_{bajo}$ el sándwich NO HABÍA sido descargada.

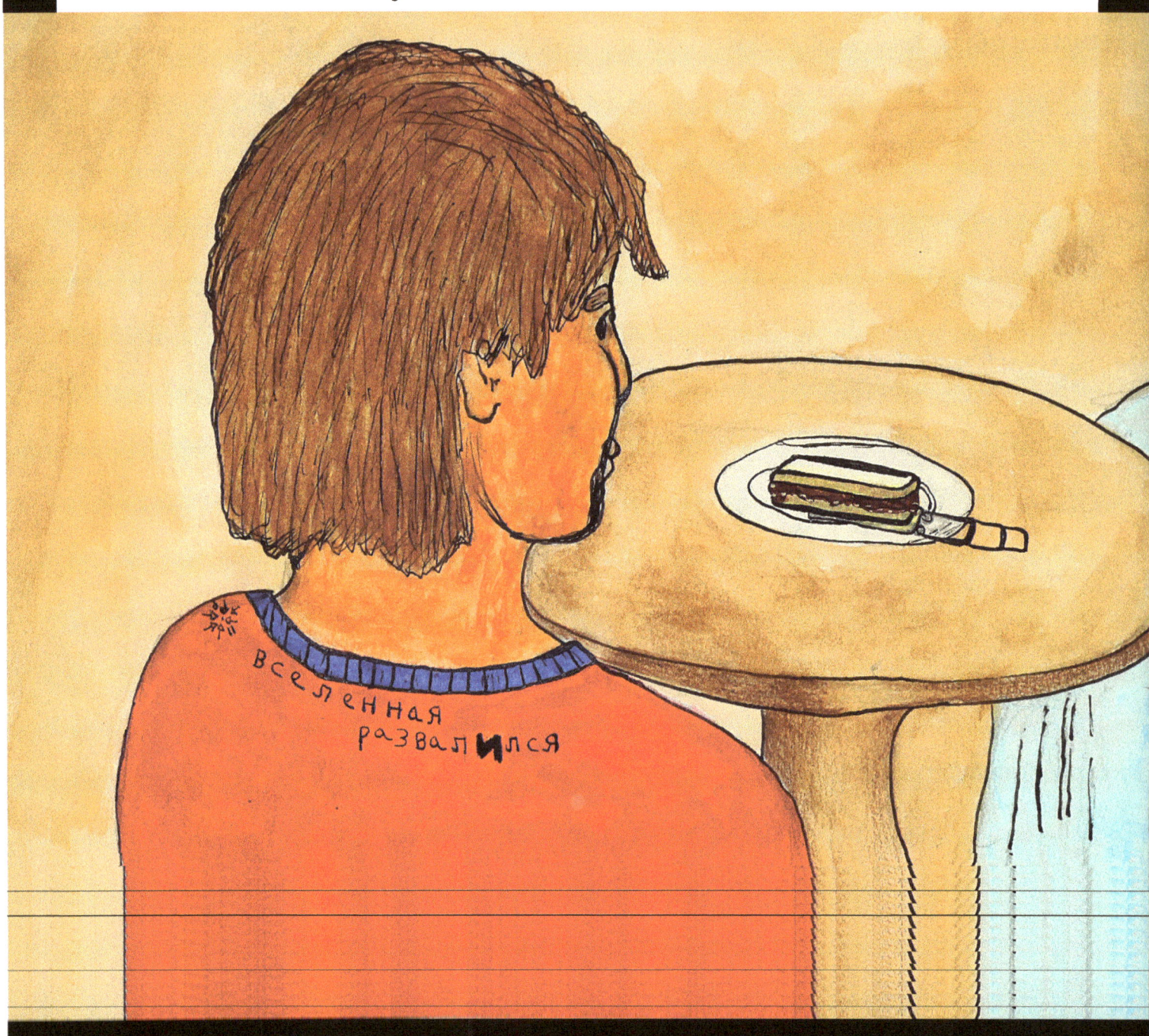

Entonces Marcos el niño DECIDIÓ **esconderse** entre la puerta y la cómoda y ESPERAR al **ladrón**

Marcos el niño ESPERO, ESPERO y ESPERO. Esperó tanto tiempo que se *d u r m i ó*.... ["pues" [[como dicen los Mexicanos]] ¡tenía sueño!:)]

Unas horas más tarde se **DESPERTÓ** el niño. Marcos estaba un poco hambriento, así que cuando VIO el sándwich en la mesita de madera, lo ALCANZÓ Ó Ó Ó Ó Ó.

Cuando el niño tomó el bocadillo, la **trampa** se ¡activó! y la varilla de acero de la trampa ¡cayó sobre sus dedos¡ "¡¡¡OUCH!!!" Marcos gritó ¡MUY ALTO! Se había olvidado de la **trampa** que había colocado **debajo** del sándwich.

Cuando la madre de Marcos oyó el grito, subió CORRIENDO las escaleras para ver qué pasaba. Al entrar la habitación, vio a Marcos en agonía con la trampa FIRMEMENTE alrededor de los dedos de su mano derecha. "¿Qué ha OCURRIDO aquí? ¿Cómo te hiciste esto a ti mismo? "Cuando su madre quitó [¿de Ecuador?] la **trampa**, Marcos se sintió mejor.[¡felicidades Marcos!:)] "Lo siento mamá, cometí un error. Preparé una trampa para atrapar al ladrón que ha estado comiendo mis sándwiches de jalea. Pero **nunca** llegó. Y mientras esperaba, me quedé dormido. Cuando me desperté estaba hambriento y cogí mi sándwich: no recordaba la **trampa** que había colocado en él.

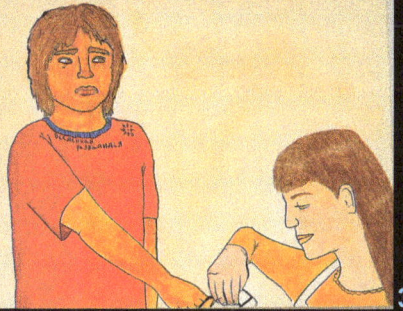

Al día siguiente Marcos el niño comió su sándwich en la mesa de la cocina. Él y su madre habían decidido, *juntos*, que era mejor para él comer su sándwich de jalea en la cocina ANTES de subir a su habitación.

Muchos días habían pasado, la **araña** blanca se hizo más HAMBRIENTA y **más** HAMBRIENTA. Como **no había más** comida en la habitación, no tenía nada que comer. Tenía que hacer ¡alGO!

Julián la araña Pensó en el asunto. ¡¡¡ PIENSA PIENSA PIENSA!!! Finalmente, se le ocurrió un idea. "Necesito SALIR de la habitación y buscar comida en **otro** *lugar*" [¿donde? ¡**otro**!:) SÍ **:)**].

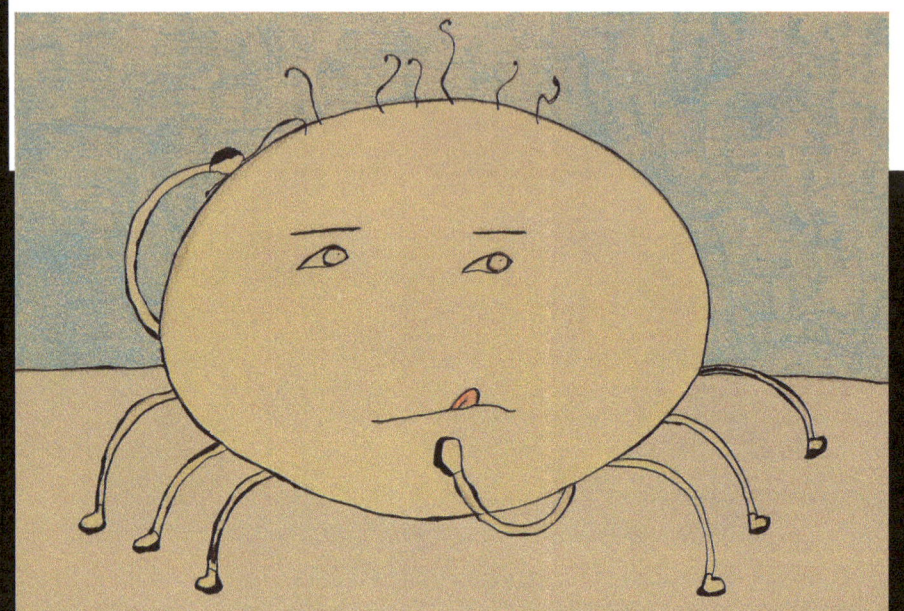

Julián decidió que esta idea era lo mejor que podía hacer y así ¡lo hizo! ¡Sí!

Sa**lió** de la caja y se dirigió hacia la ventana para comenzar su *Aventura*. [¡Excelente Julián!:) ¡Sí! :)]

Esperaba que pudiera tener **SUERTE** y encontrar un LUGAR que tuviera su comida favorita:

¡UN SÁNDWICH DE JALEA DE FRESA EN PAN BLANCO!:)

[¡Que rico mai! {{¡que Viva Costa Rica y Colombia y todo Latino América!:)}}]

El Fin.

"Gracias lector por tomarse el tiempo para leer una historia de parte de mi vida!

¡Te deseo mucha paz y felicidad siempre!"

Los mejores deseos,

Julián

www.ingramcontent.com/pod-product-compliance
Lightning Source LLC
Chambersburg PA
CBHW061147010526
44118CB00026B/2902